Explore
Tucson
OUTDOORS

HIKING
BIKING
& MORE

Karen Krebbs

MENASHA RIDGE PRESS
Your Guide to the Outdoors Since 1982

T0166271

ABOUT THE AUTHOR

Karen Krebbs worked at the Arizona-Sonora Desert Museum for more than 26 years and has extensive knowledge of birds, mammals, plants, reptiles, insects, deserts, and animal adaptations and behavior. Karen is an avid hiker, camper, photographer, and natural history traveler. She has lived in Tucson for more than 50 years.

Explore Tucson Outdoors: Your Guide to Hiking, Biking, and More

Copyright © 2018 by Karen Krebbs

All rights reserved

Published by Menasha Ridge Press

Distributed by Publishers Group West

Printed in China

First edition, first printing

ISBN 978-1-63404-118-8; eISBN 978-1-63404-119-5; LCCN 2017025308

Design: Lora Westberg

Photos: By the author unless otherwise noted

Copy editors: Tim Jackson and Clair Suer

Proofreader: Emily Beaumont

Menasha Ridge Press

An imprint of AdventureKEEN

2204 First Ave. S., Ste. 102

Birmingham, Alabama 35233

Visit menasharidge.com for a complete listing of our books and for ordering information. Contact us at our website, at facebook.com/menasharidge, or at twitter.com/menasharidge with questions or comments. To find out more about who we are and what we're doing, visit our blog, blog.menasharidge.com.

Photo credits

Front cover: Saguaro National Park by Karen Krebbs

Brian Ong: Blackett's Ridge Trail **Jena Persico:** Tohono Chul **Russell Porth:** Brown Mountain Trail

Introduction

Tucson is a dream for lovers of the outdoors. The Sonoran Desert is home to majestic plants, such as the saguaro, as well as unique animals, including the coyote, javelina, rattlesnake, Gila monster, and numerous others. Tucson's average of 300 days of sunshine per year makes walking, hiking, jogging, bicycling, and birding possible almost daily.

Numerous walking paths and trails extend throughout the city and surrounding areas. The desert is a comfortable place to walk and hike in the winter, but hiking should be limited in the summer because temperatures can quickly exceed 110 degrees. In the summer, walks should be enjoyed in the early hours—or later in the day—when the temperatures are not excessive. Parks are a good decision for the hot summer days.

Always walk or hike with water (1 gallon per person), and keep in mind that you are a visitor to a desert. Sunscreen and hats are recommended. It is recommended that you carry a compass, backpack, binoculars, and a cell phone—and that you wear sturdy shoes and layers of clothes. The Sonoran Desert is an exciting adventure, and all efforts should be made to have an enjoyable visit to this unique area.

While many of the locations featured in this book are suitable for multiple outdoors activities, if the area is especially known for one or two specific pursuits, we've listed them on the page using the indicators that you see to the right.

`HIKING`
`BIKING`
`SWIMMING`

Brown Mountain

ARIZONA-SONORA DESERT MUSEUM

The Arizona-Sonora Desert Museum is a living natural history museum, zoo, botanical garden, aquarium, education center, and art gallery.

Difficulty: Easy

Length/Time: 2 miles of walking paths over a developed 21 acres; 2-4 hours, depending on how long you spend at the exhibits

Hours/Fees: 8:30 a.m.-5 p.m. October-February; 7:30 a.m.-5 p.m. March-September; 7:30 a.m.-5 p.m. June-August (Sunday-Friday) and 7:30 a.m.-10 p.m. (Saturday); Adults, $20.50; Seniors (65+), $18.50; Ages 3-12, $8; Military, $16.50; Arizona and Sonora Residents (13+), $15.50

Getting There: *2021 N. Kinney Rd.* GPS: N32° 14.6408', W111° 10.0904'

Contact: 520-883-2702; desertmuseum.org

Additional Information: The Desert Museum was created in 1952 and covers 98 acres. The museum focuses on educating visitors about natural history and preservation of the plants and animals of the Sonoran Desert and surrounding habitats. The naturalistic exhibits for animals represent the environment that would actually occur in the wild for these animals. More than 230 animal species, 12,370 animals, and 1,200 different types of plants are featured. ♿

Exhibits include Life on the Rocks, Cat Canyon, Life Underground, Desert Grassland, Mountain Woodland, Riparian Corridor, Hummingbirds of the Sonoran Desert Region, Desert Loop Trail, Earth Science Center, and Desert Garden. There is a touch tank with stingrays. The Raptor Free Flight Program runs October-April with live birds of prey. Several live reptile presentations are offered each day. The Desert Museum is open every day of the year, but September-May are the best months for walking around outdoors.

These two trails are available at Catalina State Park for birding and nature enthusiasts. Both trails make a loop and return to the parking lot. Scenic views of the Catalina Mountains and the Sonoran Desert are possible.

Difficulty: Easy (There's a brief upward climb at the beginning of the Nature Trail.)

Length/Time: Each trail is a 1-mile loop; 1-2 hours, depending on the pace and number of stops

Hours/Fees: 5 a.m.-10 p.m. daily; Fees: Vehicle pass (with 1-4 Adults), $7; Individual/Bicyclist, $3

Getting There: *11570 N. Oracle Rd.* (Catalina State Park Visitor Center) GPS: N32° 25.7825', W110° 56.0334'

Contact: 520-586-2283; azstateparks.com/catalina/

Additional Information: Both hikes are pleasant and not strenuous. Interpretive signs line both trails, and the views of the Catalina Mountains are spectacular. The trails are appropriate for families and children. The Nature Trail sign is located north of the parking lot.

Interpretive signs line the trail, as well as concrete animal footprints of common desert animals. The views include Romero Canyon and the Catalina Mountains to the east, Pusch Ridge and Sutherland Wash to the south. Benches are also available along the trail.

At the end of the trail, turn east (left) to cross the Sutherland Wash to the Birding Trail. Here, you can spot everything from Arizona's famous Greater Roadrunners to buntings, grosbeaks, and more. The Birding Trail passes through a mesquite bosque habitat and gradually climbs up railroad ties. Benches and interpretive signs also line this trail, and there are views of Pusch Ridge.

BLACKETT'S RIDGE TRAIL

This ridge hike between Sabino and Bear Canyons offers beautiful views.

Difficulty: Moderate (levels off at the top) to Difficult (beginning of the hike is steep)

Length/Time: 6.2 miles total (out and back); 3-4 hours, depending on your pace and number of stops

Hours/Fees: Sunrise-sunset daily; Fees: daily, $5; weekly, $10; and yearly, $20. National Park Service annual passes (from other parks) accepted

Getting There: *5700 N. Sabino Canyon Rd.* (Sabino Canyon Visitor Center.) GPS: N32° 18.6231', W110° 49.3528'

Contact: 520-749-8700; fs.usda.gov/coronado/

Additional Information: You'll find spectacular views of Sabino and Bear Canyons, Tucson, and the Rincon, Santa Rita, and Catalina Mountains. The heavily trafficked trail begins to the right of the bathrooms on a wide dirt path east of the Visitor Center and parking lot. The dirt path will intersect the paved road (0.4 mile). You can also walk on the paved road to the Blackett's Ridge Trail (BRT). The Bear Canyon Tram (stop #2) is available if you don't want to walk to the trail (0.8 mile). This versatility helps those who may not be gung-ho about a more intense trail. ♿ *Only for visitor center and bathrooms*

At the signed trail intersection that includes several trails, take the Phoneline Trail to the right and hike 0.4 mile to the trailhead for BRT. The trail climbs in elevation up the ridge, and the switchbacks can be strenuous. Care and caution should be taken at the trail end due to its height and steepness. You'll encounter several lookouts constructed for the views.

Note: No dogs or bicycles are allowed on the trail.

Trek along a scenic mountain ridge in the Tucson Mountains.

Difficulty: Moderate

Length/Time: 4.5 miles total (out and back); 3-4 hours, depending on your hiking speed and number of stops

Hours/Fees: Sunrise-sunset daily; Free

Getting There: Travel west on Speedway Blvd. Speedway turns into Gates Pass Rd. at Camino de Oeste. Turn right onto Kinney Rd. Drive to McCain Loop Rd. and turn left. Parking for the trailhead is on the right. GPS: N32° 13.4096', W111° 08.6750'

Contact: pima.gov/nrpr/

Additional Information: The first portion of the hike is up the side of the mountain; once at the summit, the trail continues with switchbacks and gradual ups and downs. Take in views of Old Tucson (to the southeast), Gates Pass Rd. (east), Gilbert Ray Campground (south), and the Santa Rita Mountains (south). Looking southwest, you can see Kitt Peak and the Baboquivari Mountains. The Arizona-Sonora Desert Museum is to the northwest; the Tucson Mountains are northeast of Brown Mountain.

The trail descends to the Juan Santa Cruz Picnic Area, which has a restroom and picnic tables. At this point you can return the way you came, or travel on the trail to the east of the picnic area that heads along the bottom of Brown Mountain and in the lower desert. As you hike on the desert trail and back to the parking lot, Brown Mountain is to your right and Kinney Rd. to the left. Continue on this trail to your starting point. While sometimes rugged, the views—especially at sunset—make this trail popular among the locals.

This hike in Saguaro National Park (East) begins at the Cactus Forest Loop Drive. The cactus forest refers to a forest of saguaros and is an example of pristine Sonoran Desert.

Difficulty: Easy to Moderate

Length/Time: 4.8 miles total (out and back); 3-5 hours, depending on your pace and number of stops

Hours/Fees: Sunrise-sunset daily for vehicles; walkers or bicyclists can access the trail 24 hours a day; Fees: Vehicle weekly pass, $15; Adult weekly pass, $5 (on foot or bicycle; ages 15 and younger, free); Motorcyclist weekly pass, $10; Adult yearly pass, $35; Senior yearly pass, $10; Military, free

Getting There: *3693 S. Old Spanish Trail* (Saguaro National Park East Visitor Center). GPS: N32° 10.2229', W110° 43.7266'

Contact: nps.gov/sagu/

Additional Information: The Cactus Forest Trail begins within the Cactus Forest Loop Drive. The trail is fairly level and sandy but does pass through several drainages. The Rincon Mountains are visible in the east. A saguaro forest exists within this area, though it is not as dense as it was. Years ago, many saguaros died because of a prolonged cold spell. Saguaros can endure temperatures below freezing but usually not for more than a 24-hour period.

The remains of lime kilns can be observed about 0.9 mile south of the Cactus Forest Trail north trailhead. Sonoran Desert lowlands and typical desert plants, such as saguaro, cacti, palo verde, mesquite, creosote, and ironwood trees, are found here. You'll also get nice views of the Rincon Mountains.

This is a scenic day hike through Tucson Mountain Park. The trail, which is also open to mountain bikers, is relatively level once you descend from the ridge. Typical Sonoran Desert vegetation, such as saguaro, prickly pear, cholla, creosote, palo verde, and ironwood, is abundant.

Difficulty: Moderate

Length/Time: 13.4 miles total (out and back); 6-7 hours, if you hike the entire trail

Hours/Fees: Sunrise-sunset daily; Free

Getting There: Travel west on Speedway Blvd. Speedway changes into Gates Pass Rd. Drive down the west side of the Tucson Mountain Park mountain. Parking is on the left side of the road in Tucson Mountain Park. GPS: N32° 13.0506', W111° 06.1800'

Contact: pima.gov/nrpr/

Additional Information: The hike passes through the Sonoran Desert with saguaro, ocotillo, palo verde, prickly pear, cholla, ironwood, and a variety of typical desert vegetation. Hills and peaks are visible on both sides of the trail with red volcanic rhyolite.

At the top of the pass, views of the Tucson Valley are present. The trail climbs from the parking area for 0.5 mile to a saddle (ridge) and then gradually drops to the desert floor for much of the hike. The trail is well-signed and easy to follow. Golden Gate Mountain is on the right side of the trail as you hike, and the Golden Gate Trail is on the right at the top of the pass. Continue to hike on the Yetman Trail.

You'll cross over various washes and pass the well-preserved Bowen Ranch. The trail continues to a parking area off of Camino de Oeste. Some hikers leave a vehicle at the Camino de Oeste so they don't have to hike back to the parking lot off of Gates Pass Rd. This makes the hike 6.7 miles.

GARWOOD DAM TRAIL

Here's a hike to a historical dam at the foot of the Rincon Mountains.

Difficulty: Moderate

Length/Time: 5.6 miles (round-trip loop); 3-4 hours, depending on pace

Hours/Fees: Sunrise-sunset daily for vehicles; hikers can access the trail 24 hours a day; Fees: Vehicle weekly pass, $15; Adult weekly pass, $5 (ages 15 and younger, free); Motorcyclist weekly pass, $10; Adult yearly pass, $35; Senior yearly pass, $10; Military, free

Getting There: Drive east on Speedway Blvd. until it comes to a dead end. Parking is on the right for the Douglas Spring Trailhead and Garwood Trail. GPS: N32° 14.0301', W110° 41.0022'

Contact: nps.gov/sagu/

Additional Information: This is a pleasant loop hike in the Sonoran Desert to an old dam. You'll get views of the Catalina and Rincon Mountains, Tanque Verde Ranch, and the Tucson Valley, plus you'll see several cristate saguaros, which have an unusual fanlike crest at the top of the plant.

Hike on the Douglas Spring Trail until you come to the Garwood Trail junction at 0.2 mile. Turn right (south) on the Garwood Trail and continue on this trail until you come to signs for several trails. Continue on the Garwood Trail to the southwest until you come to the Carrillo Trail. Turn left on the Carrillo Trail, and it will take you to the Garwood Dam.

The dam was built in 1948 to provide water for a ranch house built in this area. Before you reach the dam, you may observe pools of water in the drainage; these areas are popular with wildlife. Continue east on the Carrillo Trail past the dam, as well as past several steel tanks where the trail descends steeply to a drainage. The trail will intersect the Douglas Spring Trail, which will take you back to your vehicle.

This is a 131-acre urban park in central Tucson.

Difficulty: Easy

Length/Time: A 2-mile loop of paved multi-use paths winds along the edge of the park, which connects with an additional 2.5 miles around golf and recreation centers; 1 hour or longer, depending on activity

Hours/Fees: Sunrise-sunset daily; Free

Getting There: *900 S. Randolph Way*. GPS: N32° 12.5124', W110° 55.4734'

Contact: tucsonaz.gov/parks

Additional Information: Originally the park was called Randolph Park after Epes Randolph, a railroad executive and Tucson citizen. Later, the western portion of the park was renamed Gene C. Reid Park, after the first parks director for the City of Tucson, who expanded the parks system from 8 to 84 parks. The 131-acre park features two lakes, a zoo, a baseball stadium, two covered public pools, playgrounds, a dog park, picnic areas, outdoor performance venues, and gardens. There are also two golf courses, a tennis court, a racquetball facility, and an indoor recreation center. ♿

Reid Park Zoo encompasses 24 acres for 100 species and 500 animals. In 2014, an elephant calf was born at the zoo, the first birth of an African Elephant in Arizona. The dog park is named after Miko, a German shepherd who lost his life in the line of duty for the Tucson Police Department. The Rose Garden features numerous species of roses and 800 plants. Waterfowl live on the lakes in this zoo that's open year-round.

HUGH NORRIS TRAIL VIA KING CANYON TRAIL TO WASSON PEAK

Located in King Canyon, and within Saguaro National Park and on the border of Tucson Mountain Park, here you'll find views of the Tucson valley to the east and the Sonoran Desert to the west.

Difficulty: Moderate to Difficult

Length/Time: 9.8 miles total (out and back); about 5 hours

Hours/Fees: Sunrise-sunset daily for vehicles; walkers or bicyclists can access 24 hours a day; Fees: Vehicle weekly pass, $15; Adult weekly pass, $5 (on foot or bicycle; ages 15 and younger, free); Motorcyclist weekly pass, $10; Adult yearly pass, $35; Senior yearly pass, $10; Military, free

Getting There: *2021 N. Kinney Rd.* (Arizona-Sonora Desert Museum, which is across street from Hugh Norris Trail to Wasson Peak) GPS: N32° 16.2913', W111° 12.1850'

Contact: nps.gov/sagu/

Additional Information: Wasson Peak is the highest peak in the Tucson Mountains. You'll see numerous saguaros, desert cacti, and views of the Tucson valley. The Hugh Norris Trail is signed and gradually climbs up into King Canyon and then levels off before dropping down to the wash. Mam-a-Gah picnic area, with tables and a shaded ramada, is available at 0.9 mile. Below Mam-a-Gah, the trail divides (Sendero Esperanza Trail), but stay straight on the trail to Wasson Peak.

At the top, there are views of the Roskruge, Waterman, Silver Bell, Rincon, Santa Rita, and Santa Catalina Mountains. This trail is rocky and has many switchbacks, so sturdy hiking shoes are recommended. While some parts of the trail can be challenging, you'll keep going back for the scenic beauty.

Take a hike up King Canyon to see the Hohokam Petroglyphs.

Difficulty: Moderate

Length/Time: 1.8 miles total (out and back); 1-2 hours, depending on how long you spend at the petroglyphs

Hours/Fees: Sunrise-sunset daily for vehicles; walkers or bicyclists can access 24 hours a day; Fees: Vehicle weekly pass, $15; Adult weekly pass, $5 (on foot or bicycle; ages 15 and younger, free); Motorcyclist weekly pass, $10; Adult yearly pass, $35; Senior yearly pass, $10; Military, free

Getting There: *2021 N. Kinney Rd.* (Arizona-Sonora Desert Museum, which is across street from King Canyon Trail Petroglyphs) GPS: N32° 14.8458', W111° 10.0253'

Contact: nps.gov/sagu/

Additional Information: Enjoy a pleasant hike up King Canyon among typical Sonoran Desert plants and with views of the Tucson Valley. Ancient Hohokam petroglyphs grace the canyon walls. The Hohokam people lived in the deserts of southern Arizona and northern Mexico from about 200 A.D. to 1500 A.D.

The trail climbs northeast up King Canyon to the Mam-a-Gah (Deer Dance) Picnic Area (0.9 mile). Once the trail drops down to the canyon drainage below the picnic area (Mam-a-Gah), turn left (south) off the trail and hike down the wash drainage. You will come to a small concrete dam (0.25 mile); shortly past the dam, you will encounter the petroglyphs on both sides of the canyon walls. Look upward along the canyon walls to view the petroglyphs. Return to the parking lot by continuing down the drainage, or return on the King Canyon Trail and the way you came.

RILLITO RIVER PARK TRAIL

This multi-use trail runs east to west along both sides of the Rillito River for walking, jogging, cycling, skating, horseback riding, and wildlife observation.

Difficulty: Easy

Length/Time: 21.8 miles; Walks and various activities can be as short as an hour or as long as several hours.

Hours/Fees: Sunrise-sunset daily; Free

Getting There: *3482 E. River Rd.* (Brandi Fenton Memorial Park, which accesses the Rillito River Park Trail) or *4280 N. Campbell Ave.* (St. Phillip's Plaza, which also accesses the Rillito River Park Trail) GPS: N32° 16.3273', W110° 55.0778'

Contact: www.pima.gov/nrpr/parks/rillito_riverpark/

Additional Information: The Rillito River Park Trail runs from North Craycroft Rd. to west of Interstate 10, where it connects with the Santa Cruz River Park Trail. The trail is recognized for its versatility and convenience. In addition to the usual activities of hiking and biking, it's a great trail for dogs, and you'll find it useful for inline skaters and horseback riding.

The trail intersects businesses, exercise stations, shops, restrooms, and water fountains. The trail is paved and has a dirt path that runs parallel to the pavement that runners and walkers prefer. No motorized vehicles are allowed. Pima County is developing a larger network of trails called The Loop that will include 131 miles of shared-use trails through Tucson and will link with Oro Valley, Marana, and South Tucson. 🦽

Enjoy a day hike through the Sonoran Desert and to the Romero Pools and Romero Canyon. As your hike proceeds upward, you encounter different vegetation for the higher desert elevations.

Difficulty: Moderate to Difficult

Length/Time: 5.6 miles total (out and back); 4-5 hours, depending on your pace and number of stops

Hours/Fees: 5 a.m.-10 p.m. daily; Fees: Vehicle pass (with 1-4 Adults), $7; Individual/Bicyclist pass, $3

Getting There: *11570 N. Oracle Rd.* (Catalina State Park Visitor Center) GPS: N32° 25.5317', W110° 54.4633'

Contact: 520-586-2283; azstateparks.com/catalina/

Additional Information: The beginning of the hike takes you through lower Sonoran Desert vegetation and on to the base of the Santa Catalina Mountains. Bighorn sheep reside in the Santa Catalina Mountains, but the sheep are typically difficult to observe. Romero Pools will usually have water after the winter rains, but occasionally it's dry if rainfall has been limited. The pools are a popular location for hikers and sunbathers. Romero Canyon is named for the Romero family who ranched this area in the mid-1800s.

From the trailhead, hike east for 0.6 mile to the Canyon Loop Trail junction and go right on the Romero Canyon Trail, which is marked. At about 1.1 miles the trail enters Montrose Canyon, and at 2.6 miles you enter Romero Canyon. The trail follows a divide that separates the two canyons. Views of the canyons and of Oro Valley are possible. The trail begins to drop on the north side of the ridge and head to Romero Pools at 2.8 miles. Because the pools are popular with hikers, the area may be busy.

This 101-acre park contains a perennial warm spring, a pond, hiking and walking trails, picnic areas, historic sites, and a nature shop.

Difficulty: Easy

Length/Time: Less than 2 miles of walking paths; 1-2 hours

Hours/Fees: 7 a.m.-sunset daily; Free

Getting There: *12325 East Roger Rd.* GPS: N32° 16.8715', W110° 43.8198'

Contact: 520-724-5000; pima.gov/nrpr

Additional Information: Agua Caliente Park has a rich human history that dates back almost 5,500 years. Agua Caliente translates to "hot water" and describes the warm spring and pond within the park. In 1873, a ranch and health resort hosted visitors for the benefit of the springs on the property. ♿

The park was purchased by Pima County in 1984 and opened to the public in 1985. In 2009, the Agua Caliente Ranch Rural Historic Landscape was placed on the National Register of Historic Places. Naturalist-led walks are carried out on a regular basis. Large palm and mesquite trees provide shade in the park, which is popular for bird-watchers.

The park's many features include not just the perennial warm springs, but also rich species of plants and animals, views of the Santa Catalina Mountains, interpretive signs along the walking and hiking trails, and a nature shop.

Please respect the "off-limits" areas of Agua Caliente Park. Certain areas are "off-limits" as a means to protect the fragile constitution of the park's natural water source, as well as the overall beauty of the park.

This shared-use trail for walkers, runners, bicyclists, equestrians, and skaters boasts more than 40 total miles in all.

Difficulty: Easy

Length/Time: More than 40 miles of pathway along both sides of the Santa Cruz River; Walks and various activities can be as short as an hour or as long as several hours.

Hours/Fees: Sunrise-sunset daily; Free

Getting There: *4600 N. Silverbell Rd.* (Christopher Columbus Park access to Santa Cruz River Park Trail). GPS: N32° 15.4019', W111° 00.4583'

Contact: www.pima.gov/nrpr/parks/santacruz_riverpark/

Additional Information: Much of the paved trail runs parallel to a soft dirt path that can also be used for jogging, walking, or horseback riding. Because the trail is mostly flat and extremely versatile, it appeals to a large portion of the local population. The trail runs north to south along the Santa Cruz River and accesses businesses, other trails, and a variety of neighborhoods. The northern trail also joins the Rillito River Park Trail (west to east). No motorized vehicles are allowed on the trail. ♿

In addition to the Christopher Columbus Park access, as listed above, note that from downtown Tuscon you can take just about any major street west to the river to access the trail. In addition, a trailhead shared with the Julian Wash Greenway on Santa Cruz Lane offers both parking and yet another choice for a hike.

SARASOTA TRAIL

This loop hike travels around Golden Gate Mountain in the Tucson Mountain Park.

Difficulty: Moderate

Length/Time: 1.4-mile loop; 1-2 hours, depending on your hiking speed and number of stops

Hours/Fees: Sunrise-sunset daily; Free

Getting There: Drive west on Ajo Hwy. to Kinney Rd. Turn right on Kinney and drive to Sarasota Dr. and turn right. The parking lot for the trail is at the end of Sarasota and just east of Tucson Estates. GPS: N32° 11.4046', W111° 04.5760'

Contact: pima.gov/nrpr/

Additional Information: The Sarasota Trail is one of many in the Tucson Mountain Park, which is a large area within the Saguara National Park East. This fairly new trail loops around the Golden Gate Mountain. The views of the southwestern portion of Tucson are fantastic. At the peak of the trail, you can view the Tucson Valley to the east.

At the trailhead, hike east on the trail until you come to an intersection. Turn right on the Starr Pass Trail and proceed up the trail. The trail climbs to a peak. At the top, turn left and continue on the Yetman Trail. At about 0.2 mile, turn left on the trail that loops around the mountain. The turnoff is not marked, but it is the only trail that turns left. If you miss the turnoff, the path will continue on the Yetman Trail, which climbs to the Gates Pass Trailhead (see trail #6). The loop trail climbs to a peak and then drops down to circle back to the trailhead.

Because this trail lies within a much larger trail and park system, you'll find campgrounds and picnic areas nearby that offer restrooms and water.

SWEETWATER PRESERVE TRAILS PARK

This 887-acre park boasts 15 miles of trails that are enjoyed by hikers, equestrians, dog walkers, mountain bikers, and trail runners.

Difficulty: Moderate

Length/Time: 15 total miles with more than 16 different trails that vary in length from 0.1 mile (Los Rancheros Link) to 2.6 miles (Desperado Loop); 1-4 hours or more, if you combine several trails

Hours/Fees: Sunrise-sunset daily; Free

Getting There: From I-10, take the El Camino Del Cerro exit and drive west to Tortolita Rd. Turn left (south) and drive to the Sweetwater **Preserve.** GPS: N32° 16.7349', W111° 04.9195'

Contact: pima.gov/nrpr/ for more information and a map

Additional Information: You'll find numerous palo verde trees, saguaros, and native Sonoran Desert plants, as well as dams of native stone that were built by the Civilian Conservation Corps in the 1930s. Four washes cross through the preserve. Beautiful views of the Tucson Valley are available from most of the trails. The preserve protects important habitat for native wildlife and birds. You may see various wildlife, such as coyote, javelina, mule deer, cottontail, and rabbits.

Nearby you'll find both the Tucson Mountain Park and Saguaro National Park's Tuscon Mountain District with a biological research preserve owned by the University of Arizona.

Visitors are asked to stay on designated trails and to respect all natural resources. Dogs are allowed on the trails but must be kept on a leash. Map signs are provided along the individual trails.

SWEETWATER WETLANDS

An artificial wetlands developed from a wastewater reclamation project in 1996, this scenic site now serves as an educational urban wildlife habitat.

Difficulty: Easy

Length/Time: Several loop trails (0.5 and 0.6 miles) wind through the wetlands; 1 hour to several hours, depending on time spent bird-watching or viewing wildlife

Hours/Fees: Sunrise-sunset daily; closed until 8:30 a.m. on Mondays for mosquito control; Free

Getting There: *2511 W. Sweetwater Dr.* GPS: N32° 16.7820', W111° 01.2760'

Contact: tucsonaz.gov/water/sweetwater-wetlands/

Additional information: The Wetlands is a popular destination for bird-watchers, families, photographers, and nature lovers. Large trees and shrubs can be found throughout the Wetlands—an oasis in the middle of Tucson. This is an excellent location to photograph birds, dragonflies, damselflies, and a lot of other wildlife. It's also a popular area to walk. The trails are both paved and dirt. There is ample shade, and several benches are provided throughout the wetlands for resting on hot days. No dogs or bicycles are allowed.

Numerous interpretive signs describe the recharge basins, plants, and animals. Reclaimed water (recycled wastewater used for irrigation and other non-drinking purposes) is utilized at the Wetlands. Because this is a popular birding destination, the Tucson Audubon Society has several birding festivals here.

Note: In early March, Tucson Water and the Tucson Fire Department conduct a controlled burn to remove dead vegetation that could stifle new spring growth.

With a private nonprofit botanical garden, cultural museum, education center, and nature preserve, this site has something for everyone.

Difficulty: Easy (Shade and benches available throughout the site)

Length/Time: 49 acres of natural setting; 2-4 hours, depending on your pace and number of stops

Hours/Fees: 8 a.m.-5 p.m. daily; Fees: Adults, $10; Students and Military, $5; Ages 5-12, $3; Seniors (62+), $8; Members, free; Groups of 10 or more, 10% off

Getting There: *7366 N. Paseo Del Norte Rd.* GPS: N32° 20.3555', W110° 58.9038'

Contact: 520-742-6455; tohonochul.org

Additional Information: The botanical collection displays native plants from the Sonoran and Chihuahuan Deserts and includes 300 species of cacti and succulents, 150 species of shrubs and trees, and 50 species of wildflowers. Tohono Chul translates to "desert corner" in the language of the Tohono O'odham, the indigenous people of Southern Arizona. Tohono Chul is home to native birds, mammals, reptiles, and plants. Outdoor exhibits include a Riparian Habitat, Geology Wall, Ethnobotanical Garden, Sonoran Seasons Garden, Desert Palm Oasis, Saguaro Discovery Trail, Sin Agua Garden, Desert Living Courtyard, and others. ♿

Tohono Chul has a large collection of native Cereus *(Peniocereus greggii)* that flower during the night in the summer. The Exhibit House is home to several changing galleries, from large group shows to smaller, one-person exhibits. The Tohono Chul Garden Bistro serves breakfast and lunch. October-April is the most comfortable time for walking.

This collection of 16 lush gardens is located on 5.5 acres within Tucson's city limits.

Difficulty: Easy

Length/Time: 5.5 acres of paths; 2-4 hours, depending on your pace and number of stops

Hours/Fees: Gardens: 8:30 a.m.-4:30 p.m. daily, 4:30-8 p.m. Thursday-Friday; Butterfly Magic: 9:30 a.m.-3 p.m. daily; Fees: Adults, October-May, $13, and June-September, $9; Students, Seniors, and Military, October-May, $12, and June-September, $8; Ages 4-17, October-May, $7.50, and June-September, $5; Members, free year-round

Getting There: *2150 North Alvernon Way.* GPS: N32° 14.9114', W110° 54.5271'

Contact: 520-326-9686; tucsonbotanical.org

Additional Information: Open year-round; shade is available throughout the gardens. September-May are the most comfortable months for walking. The Tucson Botanical Gardens, founded in 1964, were built from the historic home and nursery of the Porter Family. The original Porter house has been renovated as a library and administrative offices, but several rooms have been preserved for their original charm. The many unique specialty gardens here include the Xeriscape, Zen, Barrio, Cactus and Succulent, Children's Discovery, Prehistoric, Native American Crops, Plants of the Tohono O'odham Path, and Butterfly gardens. ♿

The gardens were created to provide an area of beauty and peace, as well as a place for education and demonstrations. The popular Butterfly Magic exhibit has tropical butterflies and is open October-April. The gardens feature more than 4,200 individual plants.

This important anthropological and ecological research site has a long and fascinating history.

Difficulty: Easy to Moderate

Length/Time: 3 miles total (up the hill and back); 1-2 hours

Hours/Fees: Open early mornings and evenings Monday-Friday for walkers and joggers, plus all day Saturday-Sunday; Free

Getting There: *1601 W. St. Mary's Hospital* (St. Mary's Hospital is north of Tumamoc Hill.) GPS: N32° 12.7713', W111° 00.3723'

Contact: tumamoc.arizona.edu/

Additional Information: "Tumamoc" is a Tohono O'odham word for "regal horned lizard." The hill was home to the ancient Hohokam people and the earliest known Trincheras village and ruins. The 860-acre reserve has more than 460 petroglyphs and a prehistoric garden; it was also an important burial site for O'odham and Apache people. After the Hohokam people left this area more than 1,300 years ago, the O'odham and Hopi lived in this region. Researchers have carried out studies on such subjects as saguaro flowering and population dynamics, blue palo verde's dependence on riparian habitats, desert tortoises, interactions between rodents and insects, and winter annuals.

Tumamoc conducts programs for all age levels that focus on the ecology and history of the area. Lectures, classes, and special events are popular among locals and visitors alike. Interpretive signs along the road describe the wildlife on the hill. It's also a popular site for residents and visitors of Tucson. Scenic views of the Tucson Valley are available at the top of the hill.

Best For...

YOUNG CHILDREN

1 Arizona-Sonora Desert Museum

8 Gene C. Reid Park

13 Roy P. Drachman Agua Caliente Regional Park

DOGS

8 Gene C. Reid Park

11 Rillito River Park Trail

14 Santa Cruz River Park Trail

PLANT LOVERS

1 Arizona-Sonora Desert Museum

18 Tohono Chul

19 Tucson Botanical Gardens

STAYING IN TOWN

1 Arizona-Sonora Desert Museum

18 Tohono Chul

19 Tucson Botanical Gardens

CYCLISTS

11 Rillito River Park Trail

14 Santa Cruz River Park Trail

16 Sweetwater Preserve Trails Park

WHEELCHAIRS

8 Gene C. Reid Park

18 Tohono Chul

19 Tucson Botanical Gardens

HIKERS

6 David Yetman Trail

7 Garwood Dam Trail

12 Romero Canyon and Pools Trails

BIRDERS

2 Catalina State Park Birding and Nature Trails

13 Roy P. Drachman Agua Caliente Regional Park

17 Sweetwater Wetlands

WALKERS

10 King Canyon Trail Petroglyphs

11 Rillito River Park Trail

20 Tumamoc Hill

SCENIC VIEWS

3 Blackett's Ridge Trail

4 Brown Mountain Trail

9 Hugh Norris Trail via King Canyon Trail to Wasson Peak